Copyright ©Melinda Todd 2017
Melindatodd.com

You may not give away or reproduce any part of this ebook to give away. You may not change content within this book including: adding/removing information, copying pages to redistribute or for personal use. You may not claim to be the author, artist, or copyright holder. You may not resell any portion of this book.

Thank you for respecting my work.

Please share the link to purchase with anyone you like, but do NOT share the link to the actual book.

© Melinda Todd

© Melinda Todd

A special thanks to my friends who allowed me to use their pets as models for this coloring book! I hope they enjoy seeing them!
Jamie, Nicole, Jenai, and Tammy!

© Melinda Todd

© Melinda Todd

© Melinda Todd

© Melinda Todd

© Melinda Todd

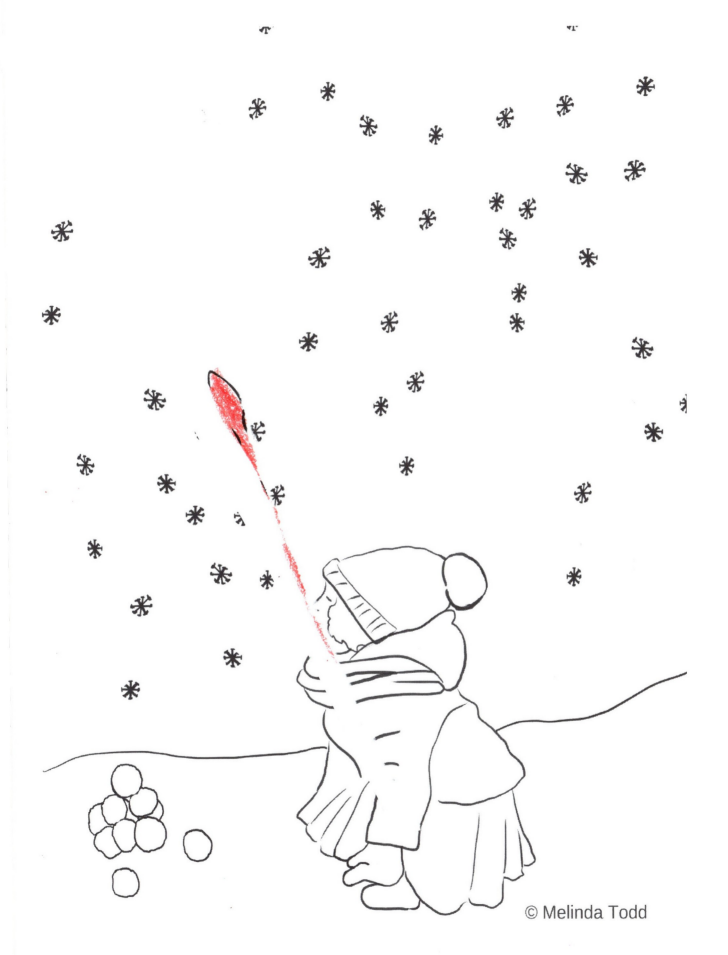

© Melinda Todd

© Melinda Todd

© Melinda Todd

© Melinda Todd

© Melinda Todd

© Melinda Todd

© Melinda Todd

© Melinda Todd

© Melinda Todd

© Melinda Todd

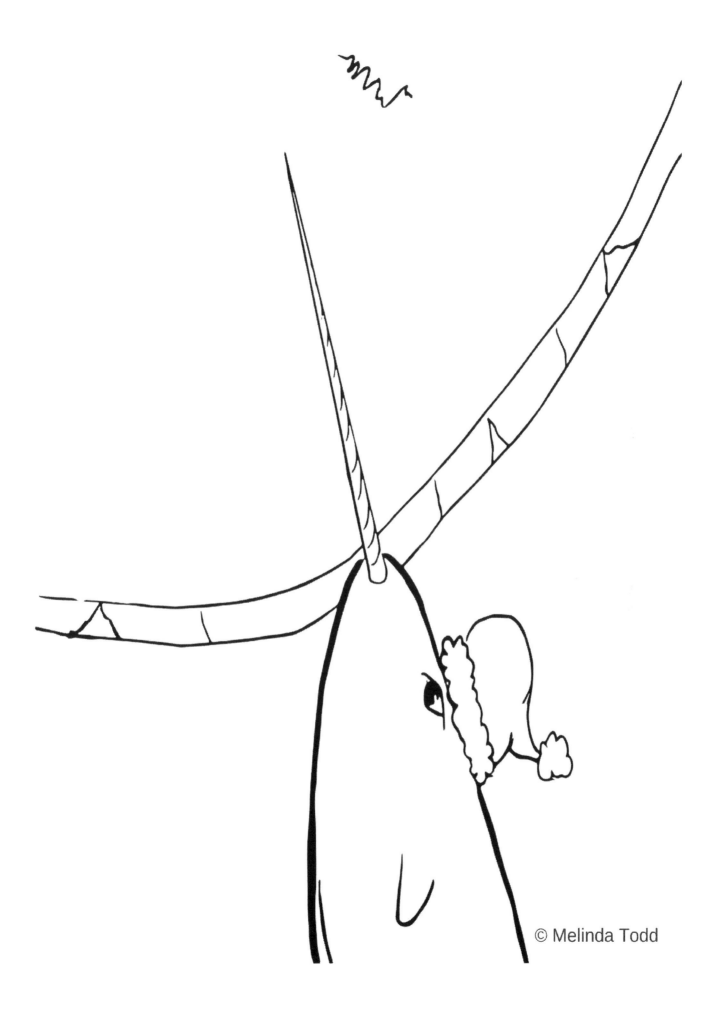

© Melinda Todd

© Melinda Todd

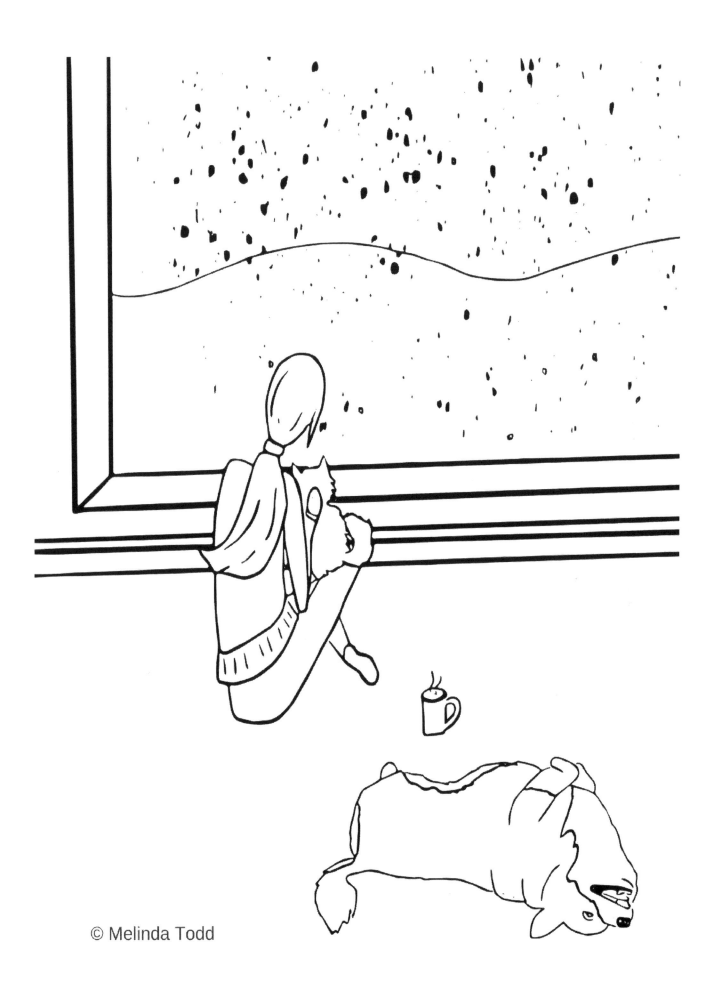

© Melinda Todd

© Melinda Todd

© Melinda Todd

© Melinda Todd

© Melinda Todd

© Melinda Todd

© Melinda Todd

© Melinda Todd

© Melinda Todd

© Melinda Todd

© Melinda Todd

© Melinda Todd

© Melinda Todd

BONUS PAGES!

More special dogs especially for Kirsten, Micah, and Martie!

© Melinda Todd

© Melinda Todd

© Melinda Todd

© Melinda Todd

© Melinda Todd

© Melinda Todd

© Melinda Todd

© Melinda Todd

Thank you for supporting my dream as an artist! Your purchase means the world to me!

Be sure to follow me on Facebook at: Mel's Doodle Designs

Instagram: Mel's Doodle Designs

And shop for mugs, blankets, leggings, socks, canvas and other prints, notebooks, backpacks and so much more on my website: MelindaTodd.com

I do commissioned work too! Contact me at melindatoad@gmail.com to discuss my prices. Let's create something unique to you.

Blessings,
Mel

© Melinda Todd

Made in the USA
Columbia, SC
22 December 2017